Making Sense of
STUDENT WORK

A PROTOCOL FOR TEACHER COLLABORATION

Kirsten R. Daehler

Jennifer Folsom

WestEd.org

Printed in the United States of America.

10 9 8 7 6 5

ISBN: 978-1-938287-12-1

Library of Congress Control Number: 2014940104

The text paper is Forest Sterwardship Council® certified.

WestEd, a national nonpartisan, nonprofit research, development, and service agency, works with education and other communities to promote excellence, achieve equity, and improve learning for children, youth, and adults. WestEd has 15 offices nationwide, from Washington and Boston to Arizona and California. Its corporate headquarters are in San Francisco.

WestEd books and products are available through bookstores and online booksellers. WestEd also publishes its books in a variety of electronic formats. To order books from WestEd directly, call our Publications Center at 888-293-7833 or visit us online at www.WestEd.org/bookstore.

For more information about WestEd:

Visit www.WestEd.org

Call 415-565-3000 or toll free 877-4-WestEd

Write WestEd, 730 Harrison Street, San Francisco, CA 94107-1242

This material is based upon work supported in part by the National Science Foundation under Grants ESI-0455856 and ESI-0455873; the Institute of Education Sciences, U.S. Department of Education, through Grant R305B070233; the Stuart Foundation; and the W. Clement & Jessie V. Stone Foundation. Any opinions, findings, and conclusions or recommendations expressed in this material are those of the authors and do not necessarily reflect the views of these agencies.

MAKING SENSE OF STUDENT WORK PRODUCTION

Production Director: Kirsten R. Daehler

Production Leads: Jennifer Folsom & Jennifer Mendenhall

Illustrator & Graphic Designer: Jennifer Mendenhall

Editor: Noel White

Publications Manager: Danny S. Torres

Proofreader: Joan D. Saunders

Production Assistant: Mikiya Alexander Matsuda

Publications Specialist: Tanicia Bell

WESTED

Chief Executive Officer: Glen Harvey

Chief Program Officer: Sri Ananda

Chief Policy & Communications Officer: Max McConkey

Director of STEM: Steve A. Schneider

Editorial Director: Joy Zimmerman

Design Director: Christian Holden

Table of Contents

Introduction

Teaching is collaborative by nature. At the center is a partnership between student and teacher. When each builds on the work of the other, the learning process hums along. The more we understand our students and their thinking, the more we strengthen this partnership and improve our teaching and, in turn, improve their learning. Closely examining the words and drawings that students create during their learning process gives us valuable clues about their thinking. Analyzing and interpreting student work reveals what they understand and where there are gaps in their understanding that can be leveraged as opportunities for growth. It reveals what to teach when and how best to help all our students make progress.

Teachers reflect on their students' work practically every day, but it's much less common to do so *collaboratively*. We've found that collaboratively analyzing and interpreting student work affords even greater benefits (and is more fun!) than examining student work alone. It is no surprise that authentic collaboration among teachers is an effective way to improve teaching and learning. Collaboration plays an important role in the education of many other professionals, including doctors and lawyers — who, like teachers, work with specialized knowledge and engage in complex decision making.

A clear structure can help tremendously in making the process of collaboratively examining student work more productive and enjoyable. This **Making Sense of Student Work** book presents a protocol that was created to help set up that structure. **The** protocol offers a detailed set of steps and guidelines for getting together with peers and discussing student work. Unlike many other protocols for teacher collaboration, no outside facilitator or external "expert" is needed! The protocol provides a framework for you and colleagues to:

- Discuss student work and student thinking in an evidence-based way
- Understand logic behind students' correct and incorrect ideas
- Strengthen your ability to make instructional choices in response to the specific ways students are thinking
- Analyze and improve the formative assessment tasks you use with students

Using this protocol with a group of colleagues provides a window into how other teachers think about teaching and learning. Their perspectives can help you broaden your own perspectives, brainstorm ideas for how to provide the best next steps for students, and problem-solve difficult teaching situations. If you and your colleagues are working to implement new standards, new curricula, or a new teaching strategy, the protocol can help you see the effects on your students and can improve the consistency of implementation across classrooms. If you collaborate with colleagues across grade levels, the protocol can help with the spiraling, or articulation, of content and pedagogy as students mature.

Who is the protocol designed for?

The **Making Sense of Student Work** protocol is designed to support groups of teachers of any subject looking together at their students' work. You can pair up with a colleague or pull together a larger group of teachers in a professional learning community (PLC), a grade-level team, or a cross-grade-level study group. This protocol is best used during the school year with current student work so you can focus on what is happening in the moment with your students and adjust your instruction accordingly.

How is the protocol structured?

The protocol is divided into five sessions, A–E. Each two-hour session has a specific focus.

Session A: Mental Models

- Interpret student work based on evidence found in that work

- Identify patterns in the way students think

- Evaluate student work on the basis of specific learning objectives

- Identify what one particular task reveals about students' understandings

Session B: Learning Gaps

- Evaluate student work on the basis of specific learning objectives

- Identify various ways students might show a correct, complete understanding of a concept

- Recognize what students are missing that may contribute to errors/limitations in their thinking

- Identify learning gaps between students' actual performance and a correct, complete understanding

Session C: Next Steps

- Recognize what students are missing that may contribute to errors/limitations in their thinking

- Identify learning gaps between students' actual performance and a correct, complete understanding

- Make decisions about instructional next steps for an individual student based on current understanding

- Weigh tradeoffs of various instructional next steps

Session D: Analyzing Tasks

- Evaluate assessment tasks for their potential to elicit and capture students' ideas

- Evaluate tasks for their potential to reveal a range of students' abilities beyond "right" and "wrong" answers

- Evaluate the match between a task and intended learning outcomes

- Identify the characteristics of good tasks for student learning and/or assessment

Session E: Modifying Tasks

- Evaluate the strengths and limitations of various assessment tasks

- Identify the shortcomings of commonly used tasks

- Choose assessments that have the characteristics of good tasks

- Modify tasks so they are better aligned with intended outcomes and the characteristics of good tasks

Each session contains a detailed agenda and step-by-step procedure with focusing questions to guide your discussion. The pages of the book themselves are a place to record your ideas and reflections. This structure allows you to devote your attention to enriching discussions without worrying about the logistics.

As you work through the protocol, please feel free to modify it to suit your needs and particular context. For example, if your group chooses to focus on a complex assessment task (e.g., portfolios or video presentations), you'll need more time for the task analysis step, and if you have a large group, you may want to work in groups of three for some steps.

Because this protocol is self-facilitated, there are three distinct roles that people from your group will need to fill — *Reader, Timekeeper,* and *Recorder.* To ensure an efficient session, the Reader, Timekeeper, and Recorder should do their work simultaneously in each step. For example, as the Reader begins speaking instructions, the Recorder should begin charting and the Timekeeper should note the stop time. The following sections provide more information about these roles.

Reader 💬

The Reader takes the lead role in helping the group meet its goals for the session. This involves reading parts of the procedure out loud to set the stage, describe the flow of events, move the group along, and keep everyone on track. The Reader may also choose to ask follow-up questions to focus the conversation or broaden the discussion. As needed, the Reader helps the group make changes to get the most out of their time together. It is *not* the Reader's role to be the expert, provide answers, or summarize the group's thinking.

A shaded box with a talk bubble (💬) gives the Reader instructions. An open bubble (◯) marks the beginning of a spoken section and suggests what the Reader should say. A square (■) marks the end of a spoken section.

Timekeeper 🕐

The Timekeeper moves the group along by writing the stop time on the board, announcing when a few minutes remain, and telling people when it's time to stop an activity.

A shaded box with a clock (🕐) gives the Timekeeper instructions for communicating about the amount of time allotted for a given activity.

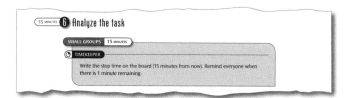

Sidebars prompt the Timekeeper to announce when participants should stop one activity and move on to another.

Recorder ✒

The Recorder's job is to keep a public record (on a chart or whiteboard) of the group's ideas at specific points during sessions. This helps everyone stay focused, revisit ideas, and build on what others say.

A shaded box with a marker pen (✒) suggests when the Recorder should record the group's thinking publicly. A sample minichart suggests a starting point for what to write.

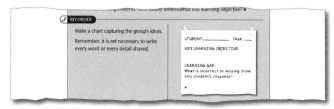

What other materials do we need?

In addition to using this guide, your group will need samples of student work, samples of formative assessment tasks, and documents that describe the learning objectives you have for students.

For Sessions A–D, your group will need to bring in student work. It's best if the group decides ahead of time who will bring in student work for Session A. At the end of Session A, you can decide who will bring in student work for Sessions B, C, and D. If multiple teachers want to bring in work for the same session, they should give students the same task. To help with coordination, a schedule is provided on the last page of this introduction.

If you are unable to secure student work for Session A (or someone forgets their work), WestEd has a few **Sample Student Work Sets** available as free downloads at WestEd.org/mssw.

For Session E, everyone needs to bring in an assessment task you plan to use with students. This assessment can be one you have used in the past or one you'd like to use with students in the future.

You will also need to refer to specific objectives you have for your student learning. You may find these in your state or district standards, benchmarks, frameworks, or grade-level objectives. Choose the document that best fits your context.

What kinds of assessment tasks are best to use with this protocol?

We've found the most productive and interesting conversations about teaching and learning take place around classroom artifacts that reveal both *what* and *how* students are thinking — and not merely their right and wrong answers. For this reason, it is key to use rich formative assessment tasks during this protocol. The following box provides tips for choosing assessment tasks that work well with this protocol.

TIPS FOR CHOOSING ASSESSMENT TASKS

You'll want to choose assessments that:

- Are well aligned with what you want students to learn/know

- Go beyond facts or simple recall and encourage students to think

- Require students to decide what knowledge to apply when

- Can be solved in a number of ways

- Give students a chance to explain their thinking and ways of figuring things out

- Ask students to communicate in several modes (e.g., words and drawings)

- Are accessible and interesting

You may find usable tasks built into your student curricula or you may need to look elsewhere. WestEd offers several **Formative Assessment Task Banks** that work well with this protocol. They are available for download at WestEd.org/mssw.

The *Uncovering Student Ideas in Science* series and the *Uncovering Student Thinking in Mathematics* series are also good resources for good formative assessment tasks (available at UncoveringStudentIdeas.org).

What kinds of student work samples are best to discuss?

The purpose of sharing your student work is to have rich discussions about student thinking with your colleagues, so it is helpful to be strategic about which student work samples you share. The following box provides tips for selecting and preparing to share your student work.

PROCESS FOR SELECTING STUDENT WORK

1. Eliminate any work that is completely illegible, promotes stereotypes, or enables individuals to be identified.

2. Sort the work into piles of students who have similar ways of thinking. This can be fun to do with a buddy.

3. Choose samples from each pile that represent students with high, medium, and low levels of understanding and show an authentic variety of responses from your classroom. Regardless of how many students you have, aim to share only 9–12 samples. This is enough to show the diversity in students' understandings and approaches, but not so many that tracking the discussion of their work becomes difficult.

4. To protect students' identities, mark out their names and assign each a unique alias (e.g., Sample 1 becomes Andrea, Sample 2 becomes Blake, Sample 3 becomes Curtis, etc.).

5. Make a copy of the samples and the blank assessment task for each teacher in your group.

6. During the session, you will provide a brief introduction to your student work samples. You can use the template on page xi to prepare. When you do this, avoid sharing your own insights.

How can we be the most productive?

In general, collaborative study groups are most successful when they operate with clear goals and shared expectations. Following are some helpful tips to make your time the most productive.

Establish an attitude of inquiry. An inquiry stance establishes an openness to questions, an appreciation for diverse ideas, and expectations for evidence-based conversations. When you talk about student work, focus on how an individual student is thinking and avoid making generalizations about how students typically think. You can help each other stay focused on evidence by asking questions such as "Where do you see that in the student work?" and "What led you to that interpretation?"

Encourage a variety of viewpoints. Sometimes the goal of a group is to reach a consensus. For example, having a shared, accurate understanding of the content you are teaching is important. However, the intent is different when analyzing student work and exploring instruction. Here your goal is *not* to seek agreement, but to share interpretations, consider alternate ideas, and explore tradeoffs. Stretch your thinking, encourage participation from everyone, and listen openly to different perspectives.

Decide on group norms. Because many people will bring in student work, it is important to develop an environment that feels welcoming and respectful. Acknowledge that it's okay to "try on" new ideas, be wrong, change your mind, and revise your thinking. Honor your beginning and ending times, come prepared, and stay focused on the learning. Session A provides a process to help your group figure out what norms make sense for you.

Rotate small groups. If you have a large group of teachers, you will spend much of the time working in pairs or groups of three. Because you learn different things from different people, mix up these small groups from session to session. Changing groups signals that everyone's contributions are valuable and each person's perspective adds to the learning of the whole group.

How was this protocol developed?

The **Making Sense of Student Work** protocol was developed by the Making Sense of SCIENCE project at WestEd. It was initially designed to be used by science teachers. In fact, thousands of science teachers and staff developers across the country have successfully used this protocol. Once these teachers discovered the protocol's powerful influence on their teaching, they spontaneously shared the protocol with their colleagues in math, social studies, and language arts. Seeing teachers across grade levels and subject areas organically embrace this initially science-specific protocol lead to the publication of this book.

More information about the protocol and the Making Sense of SCIENCE project is available online from WestEd.org/mss.

PREPARING TO SHARE YOUR STUDENT WORK

1 What assessment task did students complete? Why did you select this task?

STUDENT WORK CHECKLIST

- ☐ Select 9–12 pieces of appropriate student work.
- ☐ Mark out student names and replace them with aliases.
- ☐ Copy the samples for each teacher in your group.
- ☐ Copy the blank task for each teacher in your group.
- ☐ Prepare to introduce your student work and, optionally, copy your responses to the questions on this page for each teacher in your group.

2 What instructions did students receive about the task?

3 What did students do before completing the task?

4 What were the intended outcomes for students? What was the task designed to help them learn or demonstrate?

Having multiple teachers sign up to bring in work for the same session is a good idea in case one of the teachers ends up being unable to attend or unable to bring in samples. It works best if all teachers bringing in student work for the same session use the same assessment.

SESSION A	Date:	Location:
Presenting Teacher(s)		**Description of task or assignment for students**
1. _____ 2. _____ 3. _____		

SESSION B	Date:	Location:
Presenting Teacher(s)		**Description of task or assignment for students**
1. _____ 2. _____ 3. _____		

SESSION C	Date:	Location:
Presenting Teacher(s)		**Description of task or assignment for students**
1. _____ 2. _____ 3. _____		

SESSION D	Date:	Location:
Presenting Teacher(s)		**Description of task or assignment for students**
1. _____ 2. _____ 3. _____		

SESSION E	Date:	Location:
Presenting Teachers		**Description of task or assignment for students**
Everyone!		A task from your own classroom. It can be one you have used before or one you might use if it better fit your needs.

MENTAL MODELS

◉ Materials

- ☐ A full set of 9–12 pieces of student work for each person

  Note: There are tips for selecting student work samples in the Introduction. If you are unable to attain your own student work samples, WestEd has a few **Sample Student Work Sets** available as free downloads at WestEd.mssw.org.

- ☐ A blank copy for each person of the task that students completed

- ☐ A copy of specific objectives for your student learning (e.g., state or district standards, benchmarks, frameworks, grade-level objectives)

- ☐ Easel paper

- ☐ Chart markers in a variety of colors

SESSION AGENDA	
GETTING STARTED	**20** MINUTES
❶ Choose roles	10 MIN.
❷ Get an overview of the session	5 MIN.
❸ Decide on our group norms	5 MIN.
TODAY'S TASK	**30** MINUTES
❹ Work today's task	5 MIN.
❺ Share responses	10 MIN.
❻ Analyze the task	15 MIN.
ANALYZING STUDENT WORK	**50** MINUTES
❼ Read and sort student work	30 MIN.
❽ Compare and discuss findings	15 MIN.
❾ Identify misconceptions	5 MIN.
WRAP UP	**20** MINUTES
❿ Prepare to bring in student work	15 MIN.
⓫ Reflect on today's discussion	5 MIN.
TOTAL TIME	*2 HOURS*

Mental Models

GETTING STARTED   **20** MINUTES

---

10 MINUTES **1** **Choose roles**

WHOLE GROUP **10** MINUTES

If you are a new group or haven't met recently, take a few minutes to introduce yourselves.

If you have not yet chosen roles — Reader, Timekeeper, and Recorder — take a few minutes to read the "How is the protocol structured?" section of the Introduction, then select roles for this session.

5 MINUTES **2** **Get an overview of the session**

WHOLE GROUP **5** MINUTES

READER

This first session is designed to help us:

- Interpret student work based on evidence found in that work
- Identify patterns in the way students think about the topic
- Evaluate student work on the basis of specific learning objectives
- Identify what one particular task reveals about students' understandings

To reach these goals, we'll start by establishing some norms for our group. Then we'll work through an assessment and talk about what a student would need to know to successfully complete the task. Next we'll dig into a set of 9 to 12 pieces of student work. This will give us a chance to identify the mental models behind students' thinking. In our discussions, we'll aim to talk about students' work in terms of the evidence it presents. ∎

RECORDER

Post an agenda for today's session (as needed).

TODAY's AGENDA

Getting Started	20 min
Today's Task	30 min
Analyzing Student Work	50 min
Wrap Up	20 min

---

3 Decide on group norms

WHOLE GROUP 5 MINUTES

🗨 READER

> 🗨 Let's take 5 minutes to talk about the group norms we'd like to have.
> Group norms describe our expectations, or ground rules, for participation.
> They help us create a welcoming environment in which everyone feels
> comfortable participating.
>
> Here are some ideas to get us started:
>
> • Listen respectfully and be open to differences.
>
> • Analyze the work, but avoid judging people.
>
> • Don't let our expectations cloud our vision.
>
> • Stay focused on the evidence.
>
> • Look for what we see as interesting and surprising.
>
> What norms would we like for our group? ■

✐ RECORDER

Make a public chart of your group's norms. Revise as needed so it represents everyone's ideas.

Post the completed chart in a visible place and make sure to bring it to future meetings.

> OUR GROUP NORMS
> FOR LOOKING AT STUDENT
> WORK
>
> ►
>
> ►
>
> ►

🕐 TIMEKEEPER

After 5 minutes, call time.

5 MINUTES 4 Work today's task

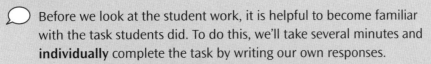

WHOLE GROUP 1 MINUTE

● READER

💬 Before we look at the student work, it is helpful to become familiar with the task students did. To do this, we'll take several minutes and **individually** complete the task by writing our own responses.

Then we'll work in **small groups** to share responses, check the correctness of our thinking, and hear different ways people solved the task. Lastly, we'll figure out the knowledge a student would need in order to successfully complete the assignment.

Go ahead and start writing your response. As you work, take note of how you approach the task. ■

Note: Distribute a blank copy of the task that matches the student work your group is working with today.

INDIVIDUALLY 4 MINUTES

a. Complete today's task. As a reminder, write your own adult-level response (not what a student would write) and think about:

- What I notice about how I approached the task…

🕐 TIMEKEEPER

After 5 minutes, call time.

5 Share responses

WHOLE GROUP | **1** MINUTE

💬 **READER**

💭 Please form a **small group** (preferably a group of three people) and begin to share your responses with each other.

You will have about 10 minutes for this discussion. When our Timekeeper calls time, please move on to the next step — analyzing the task. ▪

🕓 **TIMEKEEPER**

Write the stop time on the board (10 minutes from when the Reader begins introducing this step).

SMALL GROUPS | **9** MINUTES

a. Take turns sharing your written answers and describing how you solved the task. For example:

- Did you think of another similar situation?

- Did you draw a picture or diagram?

- Did you remember some specific facts or information?

b. Verify the correctness of your response(s). As needed, consult an answer key, curriculum guide, or other reference materials to confirm your answers.

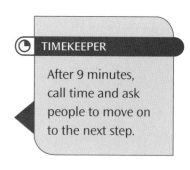

🕓 **TIMEKEEPER**

After 9 minutes, call time and ask people to move on to the next step.

6 Analyze the task

TIMEKEEPER

Write the stop time on the board (15 minutes from now). Remind people when there is 1 minute remaining.

a. Discuss the task in terms of the content it covers and take notes.

- If students correctly completed this same task, what would we know about the content they understand?

b. Together read relevant learning objectives (e.g., standards, benchmarks, frameworks, grade-level objectives), discuss which ones are best aligned with this task, and take notes.

- These specific learning objectives are a good fit with the task…

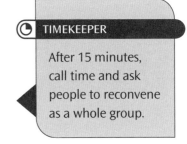

TIMEKEEPER

After 15 minutes, call time and ask people to reconvene as a whole group.

　　　　　　　　　　　　　　　　　　　　Today's Task　**7**

30 MINUTES **7 Read and sort student work**

WHOLE GROUP 5 MINUTES

READER

When we look at the student work today, we'll focus on identifying common, yet incorrect ways they are thinking about the topic. Typically, multiple students share the same mental model, or way of thinking. However, each student may express this idea differently. In later sessions, we will consider the instructional next steps that might be most fitting for students based on their ideas.

Each time we look at student work, the teacher or teachers who brought in the work will give us a short introduction to help us understand what students did and the context for their work. It is most helpful to hear about:

- Which task you chose and why

- The instructions you gave students

- What students did before completing the task

- What you hoped they would learn or demonstrate by doing the task ■

Each teacher presenting work today should take a minute to talk through these points and/or distribute your written description of these points. ■

TIMEKEEPER

Help teachers stick to brief presentations (1–2 minutes per teacher).

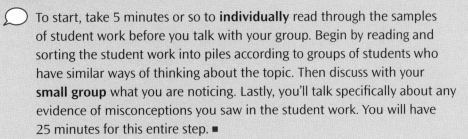

WHOLE GROUP 1 MINUTE

READER

To start, take 5 minutes or so to **individually** read through the samples of student work before you talk with your group. Begin by reading and sorting the student work into piles according to groups of students who have similar ways of thinking about the topic. Then discuss with your **small group** what you are noticing. Lastly, you'll talk specifically about any evidence of misconceptions you saw in the student work. You will have 25 minutes for this entire step. ■

Note: Distribute copies of the student work. If more than one teacher brought in work, have different small groups focus on different sets.

TIMEKEEPER

Write the stop time on the board (25 minutes from when the Reader begins introducing this step).

INDIVIDUALLY 5 MINUTES

a. First, read through the samples of student work **individually** and take notes.

- What I notice about how each student is thinking about the topic…

TIMEKEEPER

After 5 minutes, call time and ask people to move to their small groups.

b. Discuss what you are noticing about these students' ideas and their underlying mental models. Then sort their work into piles according to students who share similar ways of thinking.

Use these questions to guide your discussion and take notes:

• Which students have similar mental models?

EXPLORING MENTAL MODELS

The way we think about a particular phenomenon is called a **mental model.** Our mental models are how we imagine things work. Our mental models can be accurate, complete, and precise, but often they are not. Sometimes all that's needed is learning that missing piece of information or fine-tuning the idea. Other times incorrect mental models are built on misconceptions.

• Which ideas do most students seem to understand?

• What are some points of confusion?

TIMEKEEPER

After 15 minutes, suggest groups move on to part c.

c. Based on how students completed the task, what misconceptions (if any) do you think they may have? Take notes.

- We found evidence of these misconceptions…

 TIMEKEEPER

After 4 minutes, call time and ask people to reconvene as a whole group.

WHOLE GROUP 15 MINUTES

💬 READER

💬 There are many things to notice when looking at student work. It will be interesting to see the different patterns and common errors or misconceptions various groups identified. As a reminder, there is no single correct way to sort the work. By pointing out the specific evidence we used, such as a student's choice of words or aspects of a drawing, we can help each other understand what led us to interpret the student work in a particular way.

We'll start our discussion by having each small group briefly tell us about one of their piles of sorted student work.

In 2 minutes or less, please tell us about:

- One *category* (or pile of student work)

- The *names* of the students you included in this category

- Some *evidence* that suggests these students share a similar mental model, or way of thinking

In general, you want to talk about interesting things you noticed and different choices you made and why. ∎

✎ RECORDER

Make a chart capturing how the groups categorized students' responses.

Also document evidence the groups noticed in students' work.

Remember, it is *not* necessary to write every word or every detail shared.

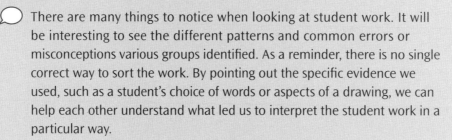

DIFFERENT WAYS STUDENTS THOUGHT ABOUT THE TOPIC...

▸

▸

▸

🕐 TIMEKEEPER

Write the stop time on the board (15 minutes from now) and announce when time is up.

9 Identify misconceptions

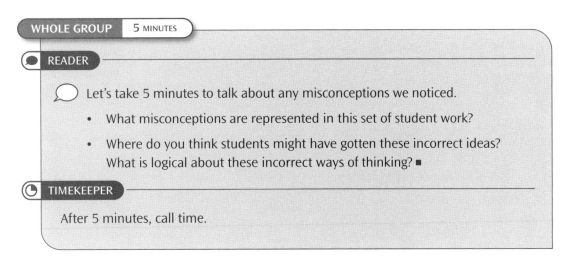

WHOLE GROUP 5 MINUTES

READER

Let's take 5 minutes to talk about any misconceptions we noticed.

- What misconceptions are represented in this set of student work?

- Where do you think students might have gotten these incorrect ideas? What is logical about these incorrect ways of thinking? ∎

TIMEKEEPER

After 5 minutes, call time.

Use this space to take notes about main points from the discussion.

TIMEKEEPER

After 5 minutes, call time.

15 MINUTES **10** **Prepare to bring in student work**

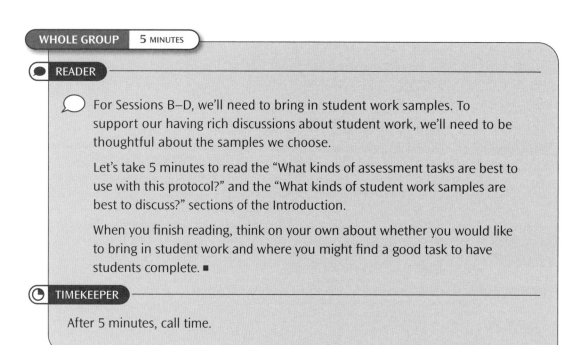

WHOLE GROUP   5 MINUTES

READER

> There are several things we need to do to prepare for our next meeting. In each upcoming session, we will take turns bringing in student work from our own classrooms. Let's take 5 minutes to talk about previous experiences we've had sharing student work.
>
> • Has anyone had the opportunity to look at student work with colleagues?
>
> • If so, can you share some highlights? What are some of the challenges? ∎

TIMEKEEPER

After 5 minutes, call time.

WHOLE GROUP   5 MINUTES

READER

> For Sessions B–D, we'll need to bring in student work samples. To support our having rich discussions about student work, we'll need to be thoughtful about the samples we choose.
>
> Let's take 5 minutes to read the "What kinds of assessment tasks are best to use with this protocol?" and the "What kinds of student work samples are best to discuss?" sections of the Introduction.
>
> When you finish reading, think on your own about whether you would like to bring in student work and where you might find a good task to have students complete. ∎

TIMEKEEPER

After 5 minutes, call time.

READER

> Please sign up to bring in student work for the next few sessions. To help with coordination, a schedule is provided on the last page of the Introduction. Keep in mind that if more than one teacher chooses to bring in work for a session, it's helpful for these teachers to use the same task.
>
> Is there anything we need to discuss to help us figure out who will bring in work and when? ▪

> Before we leave today, we also need to decide who will take on the role of Reader, Timekeeper, and Recorder next time. We could rotate roles or keep the same roles. What do you suggest? ▪

TIMEKEEPER

After 5 minutes, call time.

5 MINUTES **11** Reflect on today's discussion

WHOLE GROUP 1 MINUTE

READER

> Every session ends with about 5 minutes to **individually** think about our discussion. Give yourself the gift of this reflective time.
>
> As a reminder, our next meeting is on _____ [date/time], at _____ [location]. Our Reader will be _____ [name], our Recorder will be _____ [name], and our Timekeeper will be _____ [name]. Remember, if you have one of these roles, it is helpful to skim the session ahead of time so you know the big picture. See you then! ▪
>
> *Note:* You should also mention any other details relevant to the next meeting.

a. Take a few minutes to think about the following questions and jot down some notes.

- What were my big takeaways from today?

- What did I learn about:

    …how students think about the topic?

    …how they demonstrate their understanding of the topic?

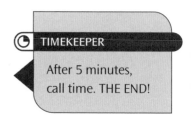

TIMEKEEPER

After 5 minutes, call time. THE END!

LEARNING GAPS

◉ Materials

- ☐ A full set of 9–12 pieces of student work for each person

  Note: If more than one person provides student work samples, it's best to use the same task. There are tips for selecting student work in the Introduction. If you are unable to attain your own student work samples, WestEd has **Sample Student Work Sets** available as free downloads at WestEd.org/mssw.

- ☐ A blank copy for each person of the task that students completed
- ☐ A copy of specific objectives for your student learning (e.g., state or district standards, benchmarks, frameworks, grade-level objectives)
- ☐ Easel paper
- ☐ 2–3 dark blue, green, purple, or black markers
- ☐ Bright red, pink, or orange marker

SESSION AGENDA	
GETTING STARTED	**20** MINUTES
❶ Confirm roles	3 MIN.
❷ Get an overview of the session	2 MIN.
❸ Discuss hopes, fears, and norms	15 MIN.
TODAY'S TASK	**25** MINUTES
❹ Get an introduction to today's task	5 MIN.
❺ Work the task	5 MIN.
❻ Analyze the task	15 MIN.
ANALYZING STUDENT WORK	**65** MINUTES
❼ Read and sort student work	21 MIN.
❽ Identify learning gaps	39 MIN.
❾ Reflect on learning gaps	5 MIN.
WRAP UP	**10** MINUTES
❿ Take care of housekeeping items	4 MIN.
⓫ Reflect on today's discussion	6 MIN.
TOTAL TIME	*2 HOURS*

Learning Gaps

GETTING STARTED   20 MINUTES

3 MINUTES **1** ## Confirm roles

WHOLE GROUP | **3 MINUTES**

Reintroduce yourselves, as needed. Let the group know if you are the Reader, Timekeeper, or Recorder. If you haven't chosen roles, quickly decide who will take on each role. To ensure an efficient session, the Reader, Timekeeper, and Recorder should do their work simultaneously in each step. For example, as the Reader begins speaking instructions, the Recorder should begin charting and the Timekeeper should note the stop time.

2 MINUTES **2** ## Get an overview of the session

WHOLE GROUP | **2 MINUTES**

READER

This Learning Gaps session is designed to help us:

- Evaluate student work on the basis of specific learning objectives
- Identify various ways students might show a correct and complete understanding of a specific concept
- Recognize what students are missing that may contribute to errors or limitations in their thinking
- Identify learning gaps between students' actual performance and a correct and complete understanding

Today we'll look at student work from our own classrooms as an opportunity to experience a new task and see how students think about the topic. After describing what students understand, we'll identify learning gaps they need to bridge to reach a complete, accurate understanding of a specific key concept. ∎

 RECORDER

Post an agenda for today's session (as needed).

> **TODAY'S AGENDA**
>
> Getting Started   20 min
> Today's Task   25 min
> Analyzing Student Work   65 min
> Wrap Up   10 min

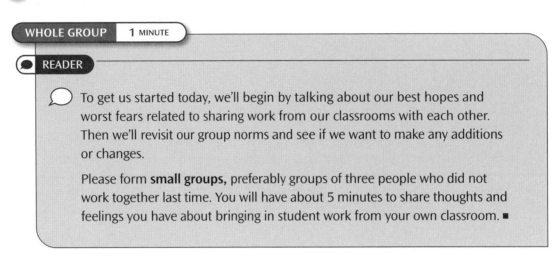

(15 MINUTES) **3** Discuss hopes, fears, and norms

WHOLE GROUP | **1** MINUTE

READER

To get us started today, we'll begin by talking about our best hopes and worst fears related to sharing work from our classrooms with each other. Then we'll revisit our group norms and see if we want to make any additions or changes.

Please form **small groups,** preferably groups of three people who did not work together last time. You will have about 5 minutes to share thoughts and feelings you have about bringing in student work from your own classroom. ∎

SMALL GROUPS | **5** MINUTES

a. Discuss your thoughts and feelings about sharing your students' work. Make sure each person in the group has a chance to talk.

As appropriate, use these questions to guide your conversation:

• What are you looking forward to as we share student work?

• What, if anything, are you feeling worried about?

• What would make you feel most comfortable when sharing your own students' work?

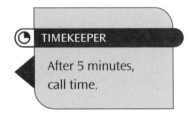

TIMEKEEPER

After 5 minutes, call time.

READER

💬 In order to make sure we have respectful and productive conversations about student work, let's briefly review our group norms. Take a minute to read them on your own.

What would you like to talk more about or change, especially in light of your conversations about best hopes and worst fears around sharing student work? Is there anything you would like to add to or change about our group norms chart?

Remember, our goal is to create an environment for collaborative learning that feels welcoming and comfortable. ▪

RECORDER

Post the chart with the norms for your group.

Be prepared to modify the chart based on group members' wishes and the discussion about bringing in student work from their own classrooms.

OUR GROUP NORMS
FOR LOOKING AT STUDENT WORK

▸

▸

▸

TIMEKEEPER

Write the stop time on the board (9 minutes from now) and announce when time is up.

Get an introduction to today's task

> **WHOLE GROUP** 5 MINUTES

READER

> Today, the teacher (or teachers) who brought in student work will give us an introduction by telling us what they had students do and very briefly sharing some background information to help us understand the context for their work.
>
> As a reminder, it is most helpful to hear about:
>
> - Which task you chose and why
> - The instructions you gave students
> - What students did before completing the task
> - What you hoped they would learn or demonstrate by doing the task
>
> Each presenting teacher should take 1–2 minutes to talk through these points and/or hand out what you've written. ■

Note: As needed, distribute a blank copy of the task.

TIMEKEEPER

Help teachers stick to brief presentations (1–2 minutes per teacher).

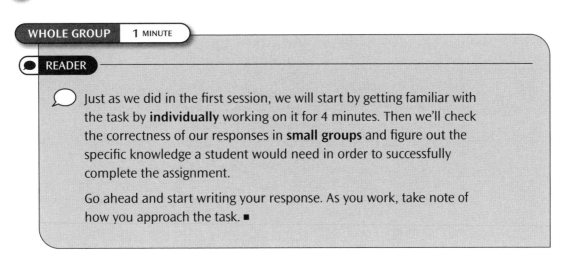

5 MINUTES **5** Work the task

WHOLE GROUP | **1 MINUTE**

READER

> Just as we did in the first session, we will start by getting familiar with the task by **individually** working on it for 4 minutes. Then we'll check the correctness of our responses in **small groups** and figure out the specific knowledge a student would need in order to successfully complete the assignment.
>
> Go ahead and start writing your response. As you work, take note of how you approach the task. ■

INDIVIDUALLY | **4 MINUTES**

a. Complete the task the presenting teacher(s) used with students. As a reminder, write an adult-level response (not what a student would write) and think about:

- What I notice about how I approached the task...

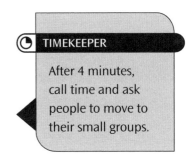

TIMEKEEPER

After 4 minutes, call time and ask people to move to their small groups.

6 Analyze the task

TIMEKEEPER

Write the stop time on the board (15 minutes from now). Remind everyone when there is 1 minute remaining.

a. Take turns sharing your written answers and verifying the correctness of your response(s). As needed, consult an answer key, curriculum guide, or other reference materials to confirm your answers.

b. Discuss the task in terms of the content it covers and take notes.

- If students correctly completed this same task, what would we know about the content they understand?

c. Consult the learning objectives (e.g., standards, benchmarks, frameworks, grade-level objectives) your group has decided to use, and identify which objectives are best aligned with this task.

- These learning objectives are a good fit with the task…

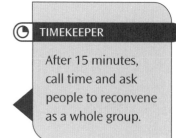

TIMEKEEPER

After 15 minutes, call time and ask people to reconvene as a whole group.

21 MINUTES **7** Read and sort student work

WHOLE GROUP   1 MINUTE

● READER

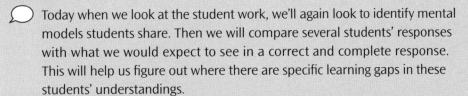

> Today when we look at the student work, we'll again look to identify mental models students share. Then we will compare several students' responses with what we would expect to see in a correct and complete response. This will help us figure out where there are specific learning gaps in these students' understandings.
>
> First, we'll take 5 minutes or so to **individually** read through the samples of work and notice how students are thinking about the topic. Then, as **small groups,** we'll share what we're noticing, sort the work into piles of students who think in similar ways, and talk about misconceptions you saw evidenced in the student work. We'll have 20 minutes for this entire step. ■

Note: Ask the presenting teacher (or teachers) to distribute copies of student work. If more than one teacher brought in work, have various small groups focus on different class sets rather than having everyone look at everything.

● TIMEKEEPER

Write the stop time on the board (21 minutes from when the Reader begins introducing this step).

INDIVIDUALLY   5 MINUTES

a. First, read through the samples of student work **individually** and take notes.

   • What I notice about how each student is thinking about the topic…

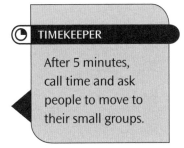

● TIMEKEEPER

After 5 minutes, call time and ask people to move to their small groups.

b. Discuss what you are noticing about these students' ideas and their underlying mental models. Then sort their work into piles according to students who share similar ways of thinking.

Use these questions to guide your discussion and take notes:

• Which ideas do most students seem to understand?

• What are some points of confusion?

• How can we sort the work so students with similar ways of thinking are grouped together?

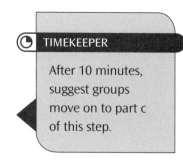

TIMEKEEPER

After 10 minutes, suggest groups move on to part c of this step.

c. Based on how students completed the task, what misconceptions (if any) do you think they may have? Take notes.

- We found these misconceptions or errors in the student work…

TIMEKEEPER

Announce that time is up and ask people to reconvene as a whole group.

8 Identify learning gaps

WHOLE GROUP | **15** MINUTES

💬 READER

💬 As a next step, we will work to figure out the learning gaps that stand in the way of individual students reaching proficiency in their understanding. A learning gap describes something a student can't yet do or doesn't yet know, but if the student could do it or did know it, his/her response on the task would be correct and complete. In other words, it is the space between a learning objective and what a student knows and can do.

We'll discuss *one* student's learning gap as a **whole group.** Then, in **small groups,** we'll look at several other students. We'll end by sharing some examples and discussing what we are noticing about learning gaps.

To get started, we first need to select one of the learning objectives or concepts that was especially central to this task. ∎

💬 Now, to talk about specific learning gaps, we need to choose *one* student to focus on. Will someone suggest a student who may not have a complete understanding of this learning objective?

With this student in mind, let's use these questions to guide our discussion:

- What is *incorrect* or *missing* from this student's response to the task?
- What *evidence* makes us think so?
- What would this student need to write, draw, and/or explain to provide convincing evidence s/he solidly understands this learning objective? ∎

✒️ RECORDER

Make a chart capturing the group's ideas.

Remember, it is *not* necessary to write every word or every detail shared.

> STUDENT:＿＿＿＿＿＿＿ TASK: ＿＿
>
> KEY LEARNING OBJECTIVE:
>
>
> LEARNING GAP:
> What is incorrect or missing from this student's response?
>
> ▸

🕐 TIMEKEEPER

Write the stop time on the board (15 minutes from now). Remind everyone when there is 1 minute remaining.

WHOLE GROUP `1 MINUTE`

 READER

Now that we have talked through one example together, take some time in your **small groups** to look at a couple of other students' learning gaps in the same way. After 10 minutes, our Timekeeper will notify us, and at that time your group should make a chart to share with the **whole group,** similar to the one our Recorder made. ▪

TIMEKEEPER

Write the stop time on the board (14 minutes from when the Reader begins introducing this step).

SMALL GROUPS `13 MINUTES`

a. Look for students who may have different mental models and therefore different learning gaps. Choose one or two students to talk about.

Use these questions to guide your discussion and take notes:

- What *incorrect* or *missing* from this student's response to the task?

- What *evidence* makes us think so?

- What would this student need to write, draw, and/or explain to provide convincing evidence s/he has a solid understanding of the chosen learning objective?

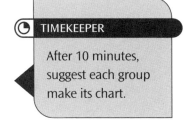

TIMEKEEPER

After 10 minutes, suggest each group make its chart.

---

b. Make a chart to share with the whole group.

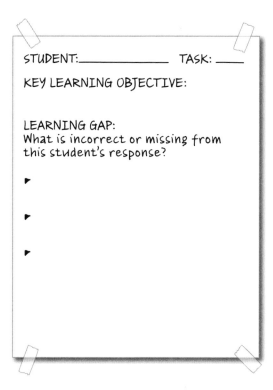

STUDENT:_____ TASK: ____

KEY LEARNING OBJECTIVE:

LEARNING GAP:
What is incorrect or missing from
this student's response?

▸

▸

▸

TIMEKEEPER

After 3 minutes,
call time and ask
people to hang
their charts and
reconvene as a
whole group.

READER

 Let's take 10 minutes to look across groups to see the various learning gaps we've identified. Each group can take 1–2 minutes to share interesting things you noticed and what clued you in to this particular student's learning gap.

It is especially helpful if you can be specific about the following questions:

- What does this student need in order to better understand?
- What evidence helped you figure this out?

Feel free to ask each other questions to clarify what you hear. ▪

 TIMEKEEPER

Write the stop time on the board (10 minutes from now). Help groups stick to brief presentations by announcing the time (1–2 minutes per group), as needed. Announce when time is up.

Use this space to take notes about main points from the discussion.

9 Reflect on learning gaps

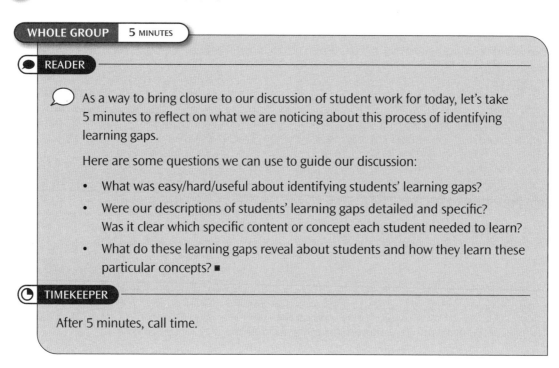

WHOLE GROUP   5 MINUTES

READER

As a way to bring closure to our discussion of student work for today, let's take 5 minutes to reflect on what we are noticing about this process of identifying learning gaps.

Here are some questions we can use to guide our discussion:

- What was easy/hard/useful about identifying students' learning gaps?
- Were our descriptions of students' learning gaps detailed and specific? Was it clear which specific content or concept each student needed to learn?
- What do these learning gaps reveal about students and how they learn these particular concepts? ■

TIMEKEEPER

After 5 minutes, call time.

Use this space to take notes about the main points of the discussion.

(4 MINUTES) **10** Take care of housekeeping items

WHOLE GROUP   4 MINUTES

● READER

> Let's confirm who will bring in student work for the next session. It's helpful to review the Introduction for more information about selecting and sharing your students' work. ▪

Note: If more than one teacher is bringing in work, ask these teachers to confer so they use the *same* task or assignment with their students.

> If you brought in student work samples today, do you have any helpful hints for teachers who are sharing next time? ▪

Read this *only* if your group is rotating roles between sessions.

> Before we leave today, we also need to decide who will take on the role of Reader, Timekeeper, and Recorder next time. What do you suggest? ▪

Note: Help the group address any logistical issues or other concerns that come up.

(6 MINUTES) **11** Reflect on today's discussion

WHOLE GROUP   1 MINUTE

● READER

> Every session ends with 5 minutes to **individually** think about our discussion. Give yourself the gift of this reflective time.
>
> As a reminder, our next meeting is on _____ [date/time], at _____ [location]. Our Reader will be _____ [name], our Recorder will be _____ [name], and our Timekeeper will be _____ [name]. Remember, if you have one of these roles, it is helpful to read the session ahead of time so you know the big picture. See you then! ▪

Note: You should also mention any other details relevant to the next meeting.

a. Take a few minutes to think about the following questions and jot down some notes.

- What were my big takeaways from today?

- What did I learn about:

  …how students think about the topic they're learning?

  …learning gaps related to this topic?

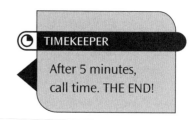

TIMEKEEPER

After 5 minutes, call time. THE END!

NEXT STEPS

◉ Materials

- ☐ A full set of 9–12 pieces of student work for each person

  Note: If more than one person provides student work samples, it's best to use the same task. There are tips for selecting student work in the Introduction. If you are unable to attain your own student work samples, WestEd has **Sample Student Work Sets** available as free downloads at WestEd.mssw.org.

- ☐ A blank copy for each person of the task that students completed
- ☐ A copy of specific objectives for your student learning (e.g., state or district standards, benchmarks, frameworks, grade-level objectives)
- ☐ Easel paper
- ☐ 2–3 dark blue, green, purple, or black markers
- ☐ Bright red, pink, or orange marker

SESSION AGENDA	
GETTING STARTED	**5** MINUTES
❶ Confirm roles	3 MIN.
❷ Get an overview of the session	2 MIN.
TODAY'S TASK	**25** MINUTES
❸ Get an introduction to today's task	5 MIN.
❹ Work the task	5 MIN.
❺ Analyze the task	15 MIN.
ANALYZING STUDENT WORK	**70** MINUTES
❻ Read and analyze the student work	26 MIN.
❼ Plan and evaluate instructional next steps	44 MIN.
WRAP UP	**20** MINUTES
❽ Reflect on our collaborative learning	10 MIN.
❾ Take care of housekeeping items	4 MIN.
❿ Reflect on today's discussion	6 MIN.
TOTAL TIME	*2 HOURS*

Next Steps

GETTING STARTED   5 MINUTES

3 MINUTES **1 Confirm roles**

WHOLE GROUP **3 MINUTES**

Greet each other and announce if you are the Reader, Timekeeper, or Recorder for today. If you haven't chosen roles, quickly decide who will take on each role. To ensure an efficient session, the Reader, Timekeeper, and Recorder should do their work simultaneously in each step. For example, as the Reader begins speaking instructions, the Recorder should begin charting and the Timekeeper should note the stop time.

2 MINUTES **2 Get an overview of the session**

WHOLE GROUP **1 MINUTE**

💬 **READER**

This Next Steps session is designed to help us:

- Recognize what students are missing that may contribute to errors or limitations in their thinking
- Identify learning gaps between students' actual performance and a correct and complete understanding
- Make decisions about instructional next steps for an individual student based on her/his ideas and understandings
- Weigh the tradeoffs of various instructional next steps

Today we will look at a new task and different student work from some of our own classrooms. This will give us the opportunity to revisit the idea of learning gaps and enable us to brainstorm instructional next steps to help move an individual student toward a more accurate and thorough understanding of a given learning objective. Because every instructional choice comes with a set of benefits and limitations, we will think together about the tradeoffs of various options.

At the end of today's session, we'll reflect on how we are working together as a collaborative learning group and what might strengthen our process. ∎

RECORDER

Post an agenda for today's session (as needed).

If you haven't already done so, post the chart with the norms for your group.

TODAY's AGENDA

Getting Started	5 min
Today's Task	25 min
Analyzing Student Work	70 min
Wrap Up	20 min

OUR GROUP NORMS
FOR LOOKING AT STUDENT WORK

▸

▸

▸

5 MINUTES
3 Get an introduction to today's task

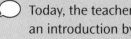

WHOLE GROUP 5 MINUTES

💬 **READER**

💬 Today, the teacher (or teachers) who brought in student work will give us an introduction by telling us what they had students do and very briefly sharing some background information to help us understand the context for their work.

As a reminder, it is most helpful to hear about:

- Which task you chose and why
- The instructions you gave students
- What students did before completing the task
- What you hoped they would learn or demonstrate by doing the task

Each presenting teacher should take 1–2 minutes to talk through these points and/or hand out what you've written. ∎

Note: As needed, distribute a blank copy of the task.

🕐 **TIMEKEEPER**

Help teachers stick to brief presentations (1–2 minutes per teacher).

4 Work the task

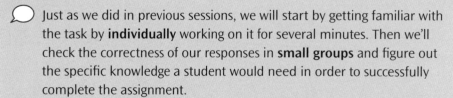

WHOLE GROUP 1 MINUTE

READER

Just as we did in previous sessions, we will start by getting familiar with the task by **individually** working on it for several minutes. Then we'll check the correctness of our responses in **small groups** and figure out the specific knowledge a student would need in order to successfully complete the assignment.

Go ahead and start writing your response. As you work, take note of how you approach the task. ■

Note: If teachers have not already formed new small groups, ask them to do so, preferably as groups of three people who haven't worked together before.

INDIVIDUALLY 4 MINUTES

a. Complete the task the presenting teacher(s) used with students. As a reminder, write an adult-level response (not what a student would write) and think about:

- What I notice about how I approached the task…

TIMEKEEPER

After 4 minutes, call time and ask people to move on to the next step.

5 **Analyze the task**

SMALL GROUPS | 15 MINUTES

🕐 TIMEKEEPER

Write the stop time on the board (15 minutes from now). Remind everyone when there is 1 minute remaining.

a. Take turns sharing your written answers and verifying the correctness of your response(s). As needed, consult an answer key, curriculum guide, or other reference materials to confirm your answers.

b. Discuss the task in terms of the content it covers and take notes.

- If students correctly completed this same task, what would we know about the content they understand?

c. Consult the learning objectives (e.g., standards, benchmarks, frameworks, grade-level objectives) your group has decided to use, and identify which objectives are best aligned with this task.

- These learning objectives are a good fit with the task…

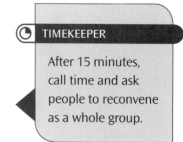

🕐 TIMEKEEPER

After 15 minutes, call time and ask people to reconvene as a whole group.

26 MINUTES **6 Read and analyze the student work**

WHOLE GROUP | 1 MINUTE

● **READER**

💬 Today we'll look at the student work with an eye to how these students are thinking about the topic and identify specific learning gaps individuals may have in their understanding. Then we will look at one student's work, brainstorm possible instructional next steps, and evaluate several options.

First, we'll take 5 minutes or so to **individually** read through the samples of work and notice how students are thinking about the topic. Then, as **small groups,** we'll share what we're noticing, discuss students' correct and incorrect ideas, and talk about the learning gaps. We will have 25 minutes for this entire step. ∎

Note: Ask the presenting teacher (or teachers) to distribute copies of student work. If more than one teacher brought in work, have various small groups focus on different class sets rather than having everyone look at everything.

🕐 **TIMEKEEPER**

Write the stop time on the board (26 minutes from when the Reader begins introducing this step).

INDIVIDUALLY | 5 MINUTES

a. First, read through the samples of student work **individually** and take notes.

- What I notice about how each student is thinking about the topic…

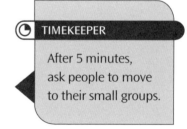

🕐 TIMEKEEPER

After 5 minutes, ask people to move to their small groups.

b. Choose a few pieces of student work that are especially interesting. Discuss what you are noticing about these students' correct and incorrect ideas.

Use these questions to guide your discussion and take notes:

- What are some things these students seem to understand?

- What are some misconceptions or points of confusion?

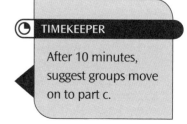

TIMEKEEPER

After 10 minutes, suggest groups move on to part c.

c. Talk about the learning gaps you are noticing. As a reminder, a learning gap describes something a student can't yet do or doesn't yet know, but if the student could do or did know it, his/her response on the task would be correct and complete.

Use these questions to guide your discussion and take notes:

- Which learning objective or concept is especially central to this task?

- What is incorrect or missing from this student's response to the task that is related to the learning objective?

- What would this student need to write, draw, and/or explain to provide convincing evidence that s/he has a solid understanding of the chosen key concept?

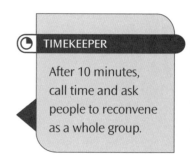

TIMEKEEPER

After 10 minutes, call time and ask people to reconvene as a whole group.

7 Plan and evaluate instructional next steps

WHOLE GROUP   5 MINUTES

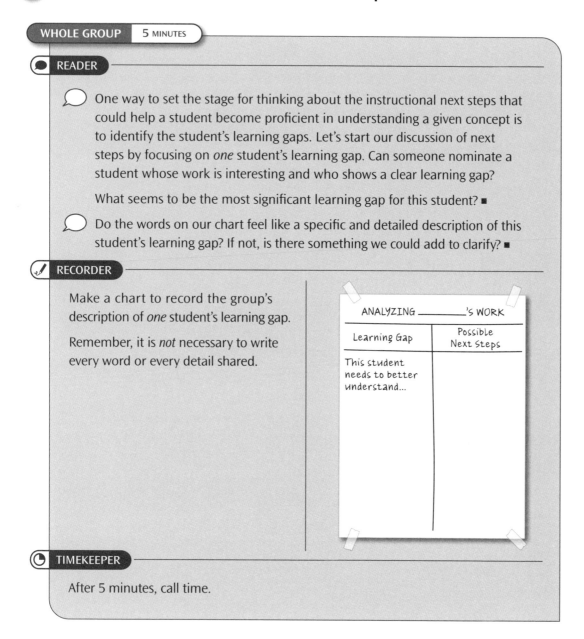

READER

One way to set the stage for thinking about the instructional next steps that could help a student become proficient in understanding a given concept is to identify the student's learning gaps. Let's start our discussion of next steps by focusing on *one* student's learning gap. Can someone nominate a student whose work is interesting and who shows a clear learning gap?

What seems to be the most significant learning gap for this student? ▪

Do the words on our chart feel like a specific and detailed description of this student's learning gap? If not, is there something we could add to clarify? ▪

RECORDER

Make a chart to record the group's description of *one* student's learning gap.

Remember, it is *not* necessary to write every word or every detail shared.

> ANALYZING _____'S WORK
>
> | Learning Gap | Possible Next Steps |
> |---|---|
> | This student needs to better understand... | |

TIMEKEEPER

After 5 minutes, call time.

Use this space to take notes about main points from the discussion.

READER

Next we'll think about how to help this one student move toward a more accurate and thorough understanding of the learning objective. In your **small groups,** take 5 minutes to brainstorm possible next steps. During this brainstorming stage, all ideas are valid and should be received without judgment. However, it is extremely helpful to be as detailed and specific as possible when describing your ideas to each other. For example, rather than saying, "I would have the student do a hands-on assignment," it is better to describe *exactly* what you would have the student do, observe, or compare. After you come up with ideas, we'll weigh the tradeoffs of some. ■

SMALL GROUPS 5 MINUTES

a. Brainstorm some possible next steps. Go crazy. Have fun!

Use these questions to prompt each other to clarify or elaborate on an idea:

- What would this look like in your classroom?
- What exactly would you say/do?
- What would the student do?

 TIMEKEEPER

After 5 minutes, call time and ask people to reconvene as a whole group.

READER

💬 Let's discuss some of our ideas about next steps in more detail.

- What is one good idea you heard someone else in your group share as a possible next step? Does anyone have a clarifying question about this idea?
- What is a different idea someone heard? Any clarifying questions?
- How about a third idea? Any clarifying questions? ∎

Note: It is important to take the time to hear a full description of each idea presented. The goal is to help the group paint a picture so people can clearly understand what the teacher and student would do. It is not necessary to share every idea; rather, ask teachers to focus on a few they think are especially interesting.

RECORDER

As teachers describe possible next steps, add these options to the chart.

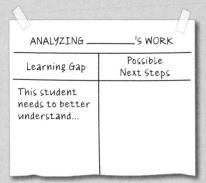

ANALYZING _____'S WORK

Learning Gap	Possible Next Steps
This student needs to better understand...	

TIMEKEEPER

Write the stop time on the board (7 minutes from now) and announce when time is up.

Use this space to take notes about main points from the discussion.

READER

Now let's think together about the benefits and limitations of these various next steps. As a reminder, every instructional choice we make comes with a set of tradeoffs. Can someone nominate *one* of these options to evaluate?

Here are some questions to guide our discussion:

- How well matched is the instructional idea to the student's learning gap?
- Does the next step build on the student's own ideas about the topic?
- How responsive is it to the student's level of understanding?
- Does the next step address what's most challenging for this student? ■

RECORDER

Make a chart of the tradeoffs identified by the group.

Although it is important to record each person's idea, it is *not* necessary to write every word or every detail shared.

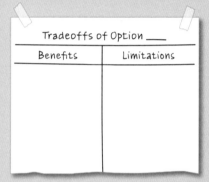

Tradeoffs of Option ____

Benefits	Limitations

TIMEKEEPER

Write the stop time on the board (10 minutes from now) and announce when time is up.

Use this space to take notes about main points from the discussion.

WHOLE GROUP | 1 MINUTE

● **READER**

💬 In the remaining time, we'll work in our **small groups** to plan and evaluate instructional next steps for another student using this same process. ■

🕐 **TIMEKEEPER**

Write the stop time on the board (16 minutes from when the Reader begins introducing this step). Remind everyone when there is 1 minute remaining.

SMALL GROUPS | 15 MINUTES

b. Choose another student whose work you found interesting. Describe the student's learning gap, then brainstorm possible next steps, and end by weighing the tradeoffs of one or more of those options. Use the following tables to take notes.

Analyzing _____'s Work

Learning Gap	Possible Next Steps
This student needs to better understand…	Option A
	Option B
	Option C

Tradeoffs of Option _____

Benefits	Limitations

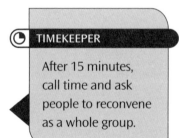

TIMEKEEPER

After 15 minutes, call time and ask people to reconvene as a whole group.

10 MINUTES **8** Reflect on our collaborative learning

WHOLE GROUP 10 MINUTES

READER

Now that we've worked together as a collaborative group for a few sessions, it's a good time to pause and reflect on how things are going. Let's take 10 minutes to think about what has worked well and what we might want to change to improve our learning experience as a group. As always, all suggestions are valid. ■

RECORDER

Make a public record of the group's comments.

Although it is important to record each person's idea, it is *not* necessary to write every word or every detail shared.

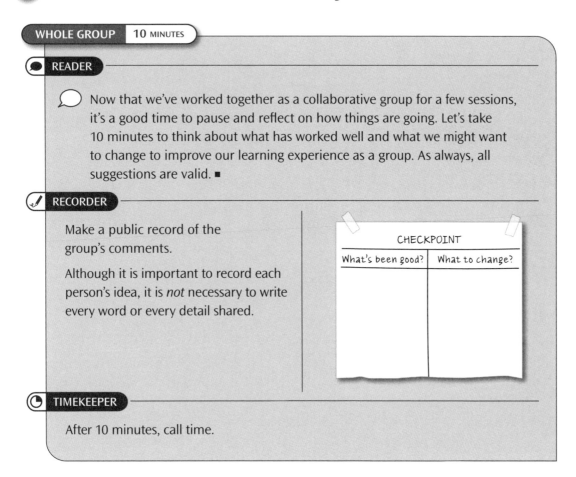

CHECKPOINT	
What's been good?	What to change?

TIMEKEEPER

After 10 minutes, call time.

Use this space to take notes about main points from the discussion.

9 Take care of housekeeping items

WHOLE GROUP 4 MINUTES

READER

💬 Let's confirm who will bring in student work for the next session. It's helpful to review the Introduction for more information about selecting and sharing your students' work. ▪

Note: If more than one teacher is bringing in work, ask these teachers to confer so they use the *same* task or assignment with their students.

Read this *only* if your group is rotating roles between sessions.

💬 Before we leave today, we also need to decide who will take on the role of Reader, Timekeeper, and Recorder next time. What do you suggest? ▪

Note: Help the group address any logistical issues or other concerns that come up.

---

6 MINUTES **10 Reflect on today's discussion**

WHOLE GROUP 1 MINUTE

READER

💬 Every session ends with 5 minutes to **individually** think about our discussion. Give yourself the gift of this reflective time.

As a reminder, our next meeting is on _____ [date/time], at _____ [location]. Our Reader will be _____ [name], our Recorder will be _____ [name], and our Timekeeper will be _____ [name]. Remember, if you have one of these roles, it is helpful to read the session ahead of time so you know the big picture. See you then! ▪

Note: You should also mention any other details relevant to the next meeting.

a. Take a few minutes to think about the following questions and jot down some notes.

- What were my big takeaways from today?

- What did I learn about:

  …how students think about the topic they're learning?

  …learning gaps related to this topic?

  …instructional next steps related to this topic?

TIMEKEEPER

After 5 minutes,
call time. THE END!

ANALYZING TASKS

◉ Materials

- ☐ A full set of 9–12 pieces of student work for each person

  Note: If more than one person provides student work samples, it's best to use the same task. There are tips for selecting student work in the Introduction. If you are unable to attain your own student work samples, WestEd has **Sample Student Work Sets** available as free downloads at WestEd.mssw.org.

- ☐ A blank copy for each person of the task that students completed
- ☐ A copy of specific objectives for your student learning (e.g., state or district standards, benchmarks, frameworks, grade-level objectives)
- ☐ Easel paper
- ☐ 2–3 dark blue, green, purple, or black markers
- ☐ Bright red, pink, or orange marker

SESSION AGENDA	
GETTING STARTED	**5** MINUTES
❶ Confirm roles	3 MIN.
❷ Get an overview of the session	2 MIN.
TODAY'S TASK	**25** MINUTES
❸ Get an introduction to today's task	5 MIN.
❹ Work the task	5 MIN.
❺ Analyze the task	15 MIN.
ANALYZING STUDENT WORK	**80** MINUTES
❻ Read and sort student work	26 MIN.
❼ Evaluate the task	14 MIN.
❽ Match learning objectives with the task	20 MIN.
❾ Identify characteristics of good tasks	20 MIN.
WRAP UP	**10** MINUTES
❿ Take care of housekeeping items	4 MIN.
⓫ Reflect on today's discussion	6 MIN.
TOTAL TIME	*2 HOURS*

Analyzing Tasks

GETTING STARTED   5 MINUTES

3 MINUTES **1** Confirm roles

WHOLE GROUP   3 MINUTES

Greet each other and announce if you are the Reader, Timekeeper, or Recorder for today. If you haven't chosen roles, quickly decide who will take on each role. To ensure an efficient session, the Reader, Timekeeper, and Recorder should do their work simultaneously in each step. For example, as the Reader begins speaking instructions, the Recorder should begin charting and the Timekeeper should note the stop time.

2 MINUTES **2** Get an overview of the session

WHOLE GROUP   1 MINUTE

READER

This Analyzing Tasks session is designed to help us:

- Evaluate tasks for their potential to elicit and capture students' ideas
- Evaluate tasks for their potential to reveal a range of students' abilities beyond right and wrong answers
- Evaluate the match between a task and intended learning outcomes
- Identify the characteristics of good tasks for student learning and/or assessment

In this session, we will shift our focus from analyzing students' understanding to analyzing tasks. This includes figuring out if a task is a good match with what we want students to learn. It also means determining the extent to which an instructional assignment or assessment is able to elicit a student's ideas and show more about the student's understanding, rather than simply show whether the student can produce a right or wrong answer.

After carefully analyzing today's task, we'll reflect on a variety of different tasks we have seen and used and will generate a list describing characteristics of good tasks so we readily know a good task when we see one. ∎

RECORDER

Post an agenda for today's session (as needed).

If you haven't already done so, post the chart with the norms for your group.

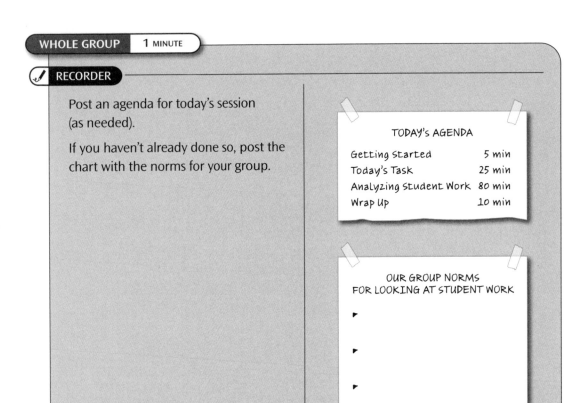

TODAY'S AGENDA

Getting Started	5 min
Today's Task	25 min
Analyzing Student Work	80 min
Wrap Up	10 min

OUR GROUP NORMS
FOR LOOKING AT STUDENT WORK

▸

▸

▸

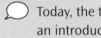

3 Get an introduction to today's task

5 MINUTES

WHOLE GROUP | 5 MINUTES

READER

Today, the teacher (or teachers) who brought in student work will give us an introduction by telling us what they had students do and very briefly sharing some background information to help us understand the context for their work.

As a reminder, it is most helpful to hear about:

- Which task you chose and why

- The instructions you gave students

- What students did before completing the task

- What you hoped they would learn or demonstrate by doing the task

For this session, it is especially helpful to hear specifics about your intended learning objectives — what you hoped your students would learn or demonstrate by doing this task.

Each presenting teacher should take 1–2 minutes to talk through these points and/or hand out what you've written. ▪

Note: As needed, distribute a blank copy of the task.

TIMEKEEPER

Help teachers stick to brief presentations (1–2 minutes per teacher).

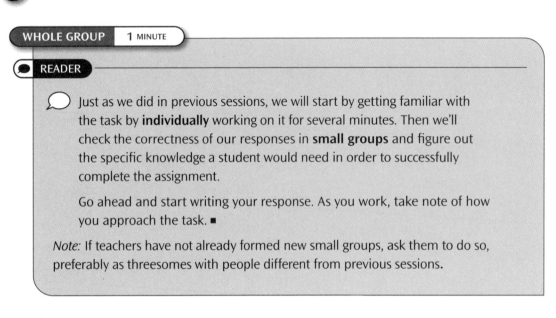

⏱ 5 MINUTES ④ Work the task

WHOLE GROUP | **1 MINUTE**

💬 READER

> 💬 Just as we did in previous sessions, we will start by getting familiar with the task by **individually** working on it for several minutes. Then we'll check the correctness of our responses in **small groups** and figure out the specific knowledge a student would need in order to successfully complete the assignment.
>
> Go ahead and start writing your response. As you work, take note of how you approach the task. ▪
>
> *Note:* If teachers have not already formed new small groups, ask them to do so, preferably as threesomes with people different from previous sessions.

INDIVIDUALLY | **4 MINUTES**

a. Complete the task the presenting teacher(s) used with students. As a reminder, write an adult-level response (not what a student would write) and think about:

- What I notice about how I approached the task…

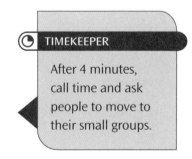

🕐 TIMEKEEPER

After 4 minutes, call time and ask people to move to their small groups.

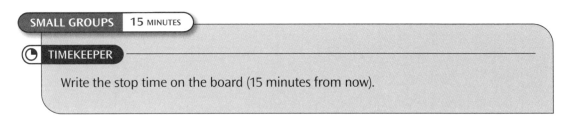

15 MINUTES **5** **Analyze the task**

TIMEKEEPER

Write the stop time on the board (15 minutes from now).

a. Take turns sharing your written answers and verifying the correctness of your response(s). As needed, consult an answer key, curriculum guide, or other reference materials to confirm your answers.

b. Discuss the task in terms of the content it covers and take notes.

- If students correctly completed this same task, what would we know about the content they understand?

c. Consult the learning objectives (e.g., standards, benchmarks, frameworks, grade-level objectives) your group has decided to use, and identify which objectives are best aligned with this task.

- These learning objectives are a good fit with the task…

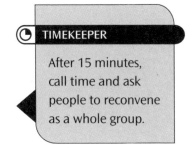

TIMEKEEPER

After 15 minutes, call time and ask people to reconvene as a whole group.

26 MINUTES **6** Read and sort student work

WHOLE GROUP 1 MINUTE

READER

Today we'll analyze the student work and the task according to several different lenses. First, you will look at the different ways students are thinking about the topic and identify their mental models and common errors. Then you will sort their work into three piles — *proficient, making strides,* and *beginning.* By looking at the work in this way, we can better evaluate the task itself.

First, we'll take 5 minutes or so to **individually** read through the samples of work and notice how students are thinking about the topic. Then, in **small groups,** we'll share what we're noticing and sort the work into three piles according to students' relative understanding of one specific learning objective. We will have 25 minutes for this entire step. ∎

Note: Ask the presenting teacher (or teachers) to distribute copies of student work. If more than one teacher brought in work, have various small groups focus on different class sets rather than having everyone look at everything.

TIMEKEEPER

Write the stop time on the board (26 minutes from when the Reader begins introducing this step).

INDIVIDUALLY 5 MINUTES

a. First, read through the samples of student work individually and take notes.

• What I notice about how these students are thinking about the topic…

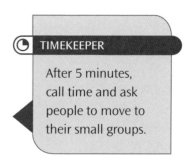

TIMEKEEPER

After 5 minutes, call time and ask people to move to their small groups.

b. Discuss any patterns you are noticing in these students' work.

Use these questions to guide your discussion and take notes:

• What commonalities or shared mental models are we noticing in this work?

• What are some misconceptions or points of confusion?

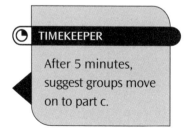

TIMEKEEPER

After 5 minutes, suggest groups move on to part c.

c. Now discuss and sort these students' work into three piles according to students' relative understanding of one learning objective.

Use these questions to guide your discussion and take notes:

- What is *one* learning objective that is directly addressed by this task?

- Does this student work indicate that the student's understanding of the learning objective is proficient, making strides, or beginning? What makes us think so?

Proficient	There is clear evidence the student has a correct and complete understanding of the *one* learning objective. Proficient does *not* mean perfect. For example, a student with a correct understanding of this learning objective may be confused about another objective or have poor spelling.
Making Strides	There is some evidence the student has a correct understanding of the *one* learning objective. There may be minor errors and/or omissions.
Beginning	There is little or no evidence the student has a correct understanding of the *one* learning objective. There may be major errors and/or omissions, along with information unrelated to the task.

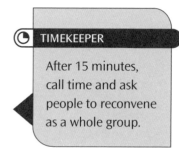

TIMEKEEPER

After 15 minutes, call time and ask people to reconvene as a whole group.

WHOLE GROUP 7 MINUTES

READER

Now let's shift our focus to evaluating this particular task. More specifically, what did the students' work show us about the strengths and limitations of this task? How well did it elicit students' ideas? How well did the task show us a range of students' abilities? What did it *not* reveal about students?

In our discussion, we can take on these topics one at a time. As always, it is helpful to support the claims we make about the task with evidence of things we noticed when evaluating the student work.

Here are a couple of questions to get us started:

- To what extent did this task enable students to express different ideas about the topic? What's our evidence?

- What did this task *not* show about students' ideas? ∎

TIMEKEEPER

Write the stop time on the board (7 minutes from now) and announce when time is up.

Use this space to take notes about main points from the discussion.

READER

A good task does more than show us right and wrong answers. When we sorted the student work by ability level — proficient, making strides, beginning — we likely learned some things about the task. In particular:

- What did we notice about the range of student responses?

- What did it look like when students had a partial understanding? Were there multiple shades of gray in their understanding?

- What does this tell us about the strengths and limitations of this task? ∎

TIMEKEEPER

Write the stop time on the board (7 minutes from now) and announce when time is up.

Use this space to take notes about main points from the discussion.

TIMEKEEPER

After 7 minutes, suggest the group move on to the next step.

8 Match learning objectives with the task

WHOLE GROUP **5** MINUTES

READER

Perhaps the most important question we can ask ourselves when choosing instructional activities or assessments is "Does the content in this task match what I want my students to learn?" Let's look together at how closely today's task aligned with what the presenting teacher (or teachers) wanted students to know.

Will today's presenter(s) remind us of your specific learning objectives? Try to state them clearly and concisely because our Recorder needs to make a chart so we can better evaluate the task. ■

RECORDER

Make a chart of the learning objectives the group identifies.

For this part, it is important to keep the language precise and detailed, rather than summarizing.

TASK: ____

LEARNING OBJECTIVES:
What I hoped my students would learn or demonstrate by doing the task...

▶

▶

READER

 Now we can analyze this task in terms of these learning objectives. Here are some questions to guide our discussion about the task:

- When we looked at the student work, what content or skills did it show these students were understanding?

- Which aspects of this task matched the intended learning objectives?

- Where did it fall short? ■

TIMEKEEPER

Write the stop time on the board (15 minutes from now). Remind everyone when there is 1 minute remaining.

Use this space to take notes about main points from the discussion.

TIMEKEEPER

After 15 minutes, call time.

9 Identify characteristics of good tasks

WHOLE GROUP 1 MINUTE

💬 READER

You have undoubtedly noticed ways in which the items in different kinds of assessments or tasks vary. Traditional tasks with multiple choice, short answer, and true/false questions and prompts are quite different from more open-ended tasks. Yet there are similarities across different types of tasks too. So how exactly do they differ?

We are going to finish our discussion today by thinking — first in our **small groups,** then as a **whole group** — about what makes a good task good. It's true that no assignment or assessment is perfect. However, by describing the characteristics of good tasks, we can be better consumers of existing tasks and/or modify tasks to make them better. ∎

🕐 TIMEKEEPER

Write the stop time on the board (10 minutes from when the Reader begins introducing this step).

SMALL GROUPS 9 MINUTES

a. Talk about what makes a good task good. One way to start is to think about some of your favorite tasks. Then use the following questions to guide your discussion.

- How are the items we've worked on together similar to and different from others you have used?

- Which types of tasks are particularly good at revealing students' ideas?

- Which types of tasks are particularly good at showing a range of understandings?

- Which types of tasks are particularly good at helping different students learn?

- What are other characteristics of good classroom tasks?

🕐 TIMEKEEPER

After 9 minutes, call time and ask people to reconvene as a whole group.

● READER

💬 To share our thinking across groups, let's take 10 minutes to do a Whip-Around in which each person says *one* thing that stood out from their discussion. We'll each need to be brief, so think about a few words or a single sentence to describe *one* characteristic of a good task. We'll go around the circle until all of our collective ideas are written on the chart (or until we run out of time). As always, you have the option to pass.

Can someone get us started? ■

✎ RECORDER

Make a chart to record the group's ideas. Write down the first example to get them started.

Keep this chart and bring it to the next session because the group will use it again to help evaluate tasks.

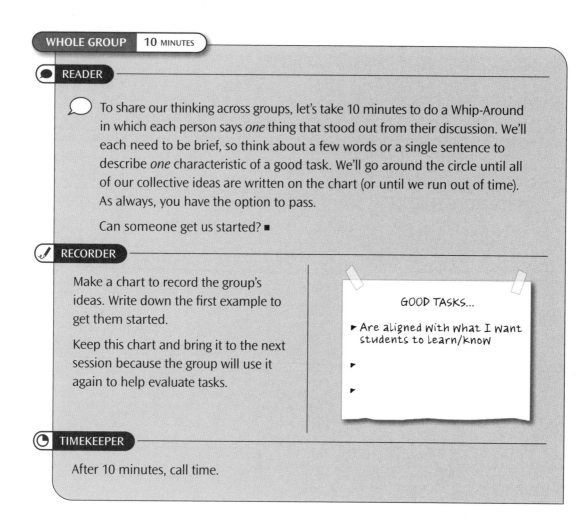

GOOD TASKS...

▸ Are aligned with what I want students to learn/know

▸

▸

🕐 TIMEKEEPER

After 10 minutes, call time.

Use this space to take notes about main points from the discussion.

4 MINUTES ⑩ Take care of housekeeping items

WHOLE GROUP 4 MINUTES

💬 **READER**

💬 The focus of our last meeting will be on analyzing and modifying tasks, so everyone needs to bring in a task from his/her own classroom related to what you want your students to learn. The task can be one you have used before or one you might use if it better fit your needs. For example, you might have a couple of multiple choice items that are an excellent match to the concepts you want students to learn, but they are limited in their ability to elicit a range of responses. Alternatively, you might have a wonderful task that isn't about the right concepts. ■

Read this *only* if your group is rotating roles between sessions.

💬 Before we leave today, we also need to decide who will take on the role of Reader, Timekeeper, and Recorder next time. What do you suggest? ■

Note: Help the group address any logistical issues or other concerns that come up.

6 MINUTES ⑪ Reflect on today's discussion

WHOLE GROUP 1 MINUTE

💬 **READER**

💬 Every session ends with 5 minutes to **individually** think about our discussion. Give yourself the gift of this reflective time.

As a reminder, our next meeting is on _____ [date/time], at _____ [location]. Our Reader will be _____ [name], our Recorder will be _____ [name], and our Timekeeper will be _____ [name]. Remember, if you have one of these roles, it is helpful to read the session ahead of time so you know the big picture. See you then! ■

Note: You should also mention any other details relevant to the next meeting.

a. Take a few minutes to think about the following questions and jot down some notes.

- What were my big takeaways from today?

- What did I learn about:

...how to elicit and capture students' ideas?

...matching learning objectives with instructional activities and assessments?

...criteria that are helpful for identifying good tasks?

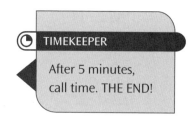

TIMEKEEPER

After 5 minutes, call time. THE END!

MODIFYING TASKS

◉ Materials

- ☐ A copy of *one* task from each teacher for each person

  Note: No student work is needed.

- ☐ A copy of specific objectives for your student learning (e.g., state or district standards, benchmarks, frameworks, grade-level objectives)

- ☐ Easel paper

- ☐ 2–3 dark blue, green, purple, or black markers

- ☐ Bright red, pink, or orange marker

SESSION AGENDA	
GETTING STARTED	**5** MINUTES
❶ Confirm roles	2 MIN.
❷ Get an overview of the session	3 MIN.
MODIFYING THE 1ST TASK	**29** MINUTES
❸ Get to know the 1st task	9 MIN.
❹ Evaluate the 1st task	15 MIN.
❺ Modify the 1st task	5 MIN.
MODIFYING THE 2ND TASK	**28** MINUTES
❻ Get to know the 2nd task	8 MIN.
❼ Evaluate the 2nd task	15 MIN.
❽ Modify the 2nd task	5 MIN.
MODIFYING THE 3RD TASK	**28** MINUTES
❾ Get to know the 3rd task	8 MIN.
❿ Evaluate the 3rd task	15 MIN.
⓫ Modify the 3rd task	5 MIN.
LIMITATIONS OF TASKS	**15** MINUTES
⓬ Identify shortcomings	15 MIN.
WRAP UP	**15** MINUTES
⓭ Reflect on today's discussion	6 MIN.
⓮ Celebrate accomplishments and bring closure	9 MIN.
TOTAL TIME	*2 HOURS*

Modifying Tasks

GETTING STARTED   **5** MINUTES

---

2 MINUTES   **1** **Confirm roles**

WHOLE GROUP   **2** MINUTES

Greet each other and announce if you are the Reader, Timekeeper, or Recorder for today. If you haven't chosen roles, quickly decide who will take on each role. To ensure an efficient session, the Reader, Timekeeper, and Recorder should do their work simultaneously in each step. For example, as the Reader begins speaking instructions, the Recorder should begin charting and the Timekeeper should note the stop time.

---

3 MINUTES   **2** **Get an overview of the session**

WHOLE GROUP   **2** MINUTES

READER

This Modifying Tasks session is designed to help us:

- Evaluate the strengths and limitations of various assessment tasks

- Identify the shortcomings of tasks you typically use

- Choose assessments that have the characteristics of good tasks

- Modify tasks so they are better aligned with your intended outcomes and the characteristics of good tasks

This last session brings together much of what we have done in the previous meetings and applies it to each of our own classrooms. Rather than looking at samples of student work today, we will work in small groups to evaluate the instructional activities and assessments we each brought in. Then we will help each other modify the tasks to better meet our needs and match the specific learning objectives we have for students.

Today we can choose to form new small groups to work with people we have spent less time with or we can work in grade-level groups or school teams to better collaborate and modify the tasks we might use. Decide which works best for you and then form your small groups. ■

RECORDER

Post an agenda for today's session (as needed).

If you haven't already done so, post the chart with the norms for your group.

Also post the Good Tasks chart from the previous session.

TODAY's AGENDA

Getting Started	5 min
Modifying the 1st Task	29 min
Modifying the 2nd Task	28 min
Modifying the 3rd Task	28 min
Limitations of Tasks	15 min
Wrap Up	15 min

OUR GROUP NORMS
FOR LOOKING AT STUDENT WORK

▸

▸

▸

GOOD TASKS...

▸ Are aligned with what I want students to learn/know

▸

▸

9 MINUTES **3** Get to know the 1st task

WHOLE GROUP   **1 MINUTE**

READER

We'll primarily work in **small groups** today to collaboratively evaluate and modify the task each person brought in. You'll get oriented to a task, work the task, discuss the strengths and limitations of the task, and suggest a few ways of modifying the task to address some of its limitations. Then you will repeat the same process with the next tasks. ■

Read this *only* if the group is working two tasks instead of three.

The times listed in your guide are based on evaluating and modifying three tasks. Since we are working in pairs and only have two tasks to evaluate and modify, we have about 14 extra minutes for each task. Feel free to use the extra 14 minutes for each task at a time when it best suits the work at hand, but keep the total time dedicated to each task about 40 minutes. ■

TIMEKEEPER

Write the stop time on the board (29 minutes from now if you are working three tasks or 43 minutes from now if you are working two tasks).

SMALL GROUPS   **2 MINUTES**

a. Decide whose task you will focus on first. Have this presenting teacher briefly introduce the task by sharing:

- Which task the teacher chose and why
- What the teacher hopes students will learn or demonstrate by doing the task

b. Write an adult-level response to this task.

SMALL GROUPS   3 MINUTES

c. Verify the correctness of your response(s). As needed, consult an answer key, curriculum guide, or other reference materials to confirm your answers.

15 MINUTES **4** Evaluate the 1ˢᵗ task

SMALL GROUPS   15 MINUTES

a. Consult the learning objectives (e.g., standards, benchmarks, frameworks, grade-level objectives) your group has decided to use, and identify which objectives are best aligned with this task.

- Which specific learning objectives or concepts does the task get at?

- Which aspects of this task match the teacher's intended learning objectives?

- Where does it fall short?

b. Discuss the potential strengths/limitations of this task. Refer to your group's chart showing characteristics of good tasks (or use the sample chart below).

Use these questions to guide your discussion and take notes:

- To what extent does the task (as it is currently written) enable students to express different ideas?

- What might this task *not* show about students' ideas?

- To what extent does the task reveal only right and wrong answers versus a range of responses?

- How might this task enable a student to show partial understanding?

GOOD TASKS...

- ► Are well aligned with what I want students to learn/know

- ► Go beyond facts or simple recall

- ► Can be solved in a number of ways

- ► Give students a chance to explain their thinking

- ► Might ask students to communicate in several modes (words, drawings)

- ► Are accessible and interesting

- ► Encourage students to think

- ► Require students to decide what knowledge to apply when

- ► Invite students to share their own ideas and ways of figuring things out

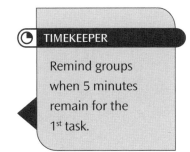

TIMEKEEPER

Remind groups when 5 minutes remain for the 1st task.

5 Modify the 1ˢᵗ task

a. Identify one or two things you would like to change about this task. Discuss why these changes would be useful. If you have time, revise the task to better meet your needs.

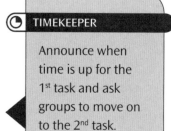

TIMEKEEPER

Announce when time is up for the 1ˢᵗ task and ask groups to move on to the 2ⁿᵈ task.

8 MINUTES **6** Get to know the 2nd task

SMALL GROUPS   2 MINUTES

a. Decide whose task you will focus on this time. Have this presenting teacher briefly introduce the task by sharing:

- Which task the teacher chose and why

- What the teacher hopes students will learn or demonstrate by doing the task

INDIVIDUALLY   3 MINUTES

b. Write an adult-level response to this task.

SMALL GROUPS   3 MINUTES

c. Verify the correctness of your response(s). As needed, consult an answer key, curriculum guide, or other reference materials to confirm your answers.

7 **Evaluate the 2ⁿᵈ task**

SMALL GROUPS | **15** MINUTES

a. Consult the learning objectives (e.g., standards, benchmarks, frameworks, grade-level objectives) your group has decided to use, and identify which objectives are best aligned with this task.

- Which specific learning objectives or concepts does the task get at?

- Which aspects of this task match the teacher's intended learning objectives?

- Where does it fall short?

b. Discuss the potential strengths/limitations of this task. Refer to the chart showing characteristics of good tasks.

Use these questions to guide your discussion and take notes:

- To what extent does the task (as it is currently written) enable students to express different ideas?

- What might this task *not* show about students' ideas?

- To what extent does the task reveal only right and wrong answers versus a range of responses?

- How might this task enable a student to show partial understanding?

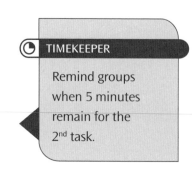

TIMEKEEPER

Remind groups when 5 minutes remain for the 2ⁿᵈ task.

8 Modify the 2nd task

a. Identify one or two things you would like to change about this task. Discuss why these changes would be useful. If you have time, revise the task to better meet your needs.

TIMEKEEPER

Announce when time is up for the 2nd task and ask groups to move on to the 3rd task.

8 MINUTES **9** Get to know the 3ʳᵈ task

> **SMALL GROUPS**   2 MINUTES

> *Note:* **Skip steps 9–11 if the group is working two tasks instead of three tasks.**
>
> **a.** Have this presenting teacher briefly introduce the task by sharing:
>
>   • Which task the teacher chose and why
>
>   • What the teacher hopes students will learn or demonstrate by doing the task

> **INDIVIDUALLY**   3 MINUTES

> **b.** Write an adult-level response to this task.

> **SMALL GROUPS**   3 MINUTES

> **c.** Verify the correctness of your response(s). As needed, consult an answer key, curriculum guide, or other reference materials to confirm your answers.

SMALL GROUPS 15 MINUTES

a. Consult the learning objectives (e.g., standards, benchmarks, frameworks, grade-level objectives) your group has decided to use, and identify which objectives are best aligned with this task.

- Which specific learning objectives or concepts does the task get at?

- Which aspects of this task match the teacher's intended learning objectives?

- Where does it fall short?

b. Discuss the potential strengths/limitations of this task. Refer to the chart showing characteristics of good tasks.

Use these questions to guide your discussion and take notes:

- To what extent does the task (as it is currently written) enable students to express different ideas?

- What might this task *not* show about students' ideas?

- To what extent does the task reveal only right and wrong answers versus a range of responses?

- How might this task enable a student to show partial understanding?

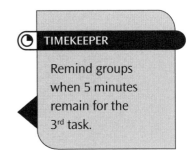

TIMEKEEPER

Remind groups when 5 minutes remain for the 3ʳᵈ task.

11 Modify the 3rd task

SMALL GROUPS 5 MINUTES

a. Identify one or two things you would like to change about this task. Discuss why these changes would be useful. If you have time, revise the task to better meet your needs.

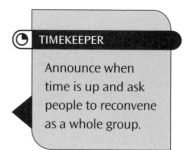

TIMEKEEPER

Announce when time is up and ask people to reconvene as a whole group.

15 MINUTES **12** **Identify shortcomings**

WHOLE GROUP   **15 MINUTES**

● READER

💬 To wrap up today's discussion about tasks, let's take 15 minutes to reflect on the instructional activities and assessments we typically see and use. The purpose for doing this is to become better consumers of the instructional materials we use with our students and to strengthen our teaching by choosing and/or modifying the tasks we use.

Let's start by taking 5 minutes to talk about this question:

- What are some limitations we often see in the instructional activities and assessments that are typically available for students? ▪

💬 With these limitations in mind, let's take 10 minutes to think about how we might improve the tasks we use with students.

- How might we modify the tasks we use to address these limitations? ▪

🕐 TIMEKEEPER

Write the stop time on the board (15 minutes from now).

Use this space to take notes about main points from the discussion.

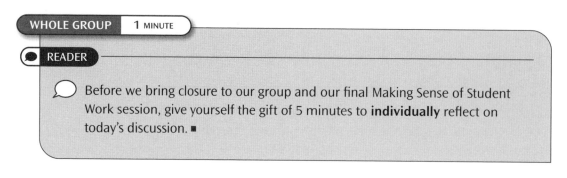

6 MINUTES **13** Reflect on today's discussion

WHOLE GROUP   1 MINUTE

READER

Before we bring closure to our group and our final Making Sense of Student Work session, give yourself the gift of 5 minutes to **individually** reflect on today's discussion. ▪

INDIVIDUALLY   5 MINUTES

a. Take a few minutes to think about the following questions and jot down some notes.

- What were my big takeaways from today?

- What did I learn about the tasks I use?

- What did I learn about modifying instructional activities and assessments?

- What are some of my overall takeaways from the Making Sense of Student Work sessions?

9 MINUTES **14** Celebrate accomplishments and bring closure

WHOLE GROUP **9** MINUTES

READER

As a way to bring closure to our time together, let's take just a few minutes to acknowledge each other, say thank you, and name some of the important things we are taking away from this experience.

We can go around the room and each person can say 1–2 sentences, for example:

- Something you want to thank the group for
- Something you are taking away from this experience ∎

Note: Also address any remaining logistical issues, such as course credit, what's next for this group, other evaluation needs, and other thank-yous (e.g., administrators, support staff).

TIMEKEEPER

After 9 minutes, call time. THE END!

About the Authors

Kirsten R. Daehler began her work in science education as a high school chemistry and physics teacher and department chair, delighting in her work with adolescents and her fellow science teachers. Upon joining WestEd in 1994, Kirsten served as the lead teacher developer and content expert for the National Board for Professional Teaching Standards. Currently, Kirsten directs the Understanding Science for Teaching project. Her goal is to transform the way teachers learn about science and the complex art of teaching. Kirsten holds a BA in chemistry from Wellesley College and an MA in secondary education from San Francisco State University.

Jennifer Folsom holds a BA in biology and has studied many other branches of science, environmental education, anthropology, and English. She began her career in science education while in high school, conducting research in a pharmacology lab and teaching K–5 students at a neighborhood environmental education center. Since then, she has worked with numerous school districts, nonprofits, and universities to conceptualize and produce innovative science curricula for students and teachers in collaboration with scientists, teachers, and science education professors. Currently, Jennifer combines her writing skills, teaching insights, and science knowledge to develop Making Sense of SCIENCE courses with the Understanding Science for Teaching project at WestEd.

Also Available from WestEd

Math Pathways & Pitfalls Curriculum

By Carne Barnett-Clarke and Alma B. Ramírez
with Debra Coggins

Math Pathways & Pitfalls (MPP) Curriculum is aligned to the Common Core State Standards (CCSS) for Mathematics in the domains of Operations & Algebraic Thinking and Numbers and Operations.

The curriculum helps students tackle stubborn pitfalls head-on and transform these pitfalls into pathways for learning key topics. With MPP lessons and instructional strategies, teachers can:

- Help students master key mathematical standards

- Support academic language development

- Prevent common pitfalls on homework

- Raise achievement on standardized tests

- Reach diverse students in the classroom, including English language learners

Each book contains everything needed to teach MPP effectively, including:

- 20–22 complete lessons

- Teaching manual

- DVD footage of MPP in action

- CD with black line masters

- Teacher professional development tasks, activities, and video footage

- Discussion Builders classroom poster

To download sample lessons and learn how student exposure to Math Pathways & Pitfalls increases mathematics achievement, visit **WestEd.org/mpp.**

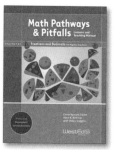
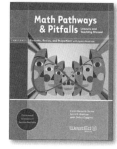
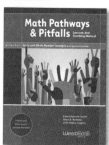

Grades K–1
$165.00 • 320 pages • 978-0-914409-58-8

Grades 2–3
$165.00 • 352 pages • 978-0-914409-59-5

Grades 4–6
$165.00 • 368 pages • 978-0-914409-60-1

Grades 6–8
$165.00 • 368 pages • 978-0-914409-61-8

For more information and to order »   WestEd.org/mpp

or call the WestEd Publications Center » 888.293.7833

Also Available from WestEd

Making Mathematics Accessible to English Learners

A Guidebook for Teachers

By John Carr, Cathy Carroll, Sarah Cremer, Mardi Gale, Rachel Lagunoff, and Ursula Sexton

This practical book helps upper elementary, middle, and high school mathematics teachers effectively reach English learners in their classrooms. Designed for teachers who have had limited preparation for teaching mathematics to English learners, the guide offers an integrated approach to teaching mathematics content and English language skills, including guidance on best instructional practices from the field, powerful and concrete strategies for teaching mathematics content along with academic language, and sample lesson scenarios that can be implemented immediately in any mathematics class. It includes:

- Rubrics to help teachers identify the most important language skills at five English-language development levels

- Practical guidance and tips from research and the field

- Seven scaffolding strategies for differentiating instruction

- Seven tools to promote mathematical language

- Assessment techniques and accommodations to lower communication barriers for English learners

- Three integrated lesson scenarios demonstrating how to combine and embed these various strategies, tools, techniques, and approaches

Chapter topics include teaching inquiry-based mathematics, understanding first and second language development, teaching the language of mathematics, scaffolding mathematics learning, and applying strategies in the classroom.

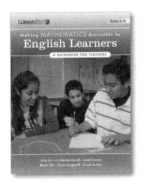

Making Mathematics Accessible to English Learners
ISBN: 978-0-914409-68-7
128 pages
$24.95

> 66 This book's clear, understandable writing style **makes complex ideas accessible.** The authors explain how teaching strategies that are good for English learners are good **for all diverse learners.** This principle is the heart of equity. 99

~Kathlan Latimer
Mathematics and Science Leadership Office,
California Department of Education

For sample chapters and to order » WestEd.org/bookstore

or call the WestEd Publications Center » 888.293.7833

Also Available from WestEd

Facilitator Guides & Teacher Books
By Kirsten Daehler and Jennifer Folsom

Making Sense of SCIENCE (MSS) offers an approach to teacher learning that combines in-depth science with a focus on classroom practice, literacy support, and pedagogical reasoning. The MSS courses prepare teachers for the new Common Core and Next Generation Science Standards. MSS supports teacher educators, staff developers, curriculum specialists, and others who work with preservice and/or practicing science teachers to strengthen their content knowledge, pedagogical reasoning, and instructional skill.

> ❝ At last we have an **outstanding** professional development **resource** that makes a measurable difference **for teachers and their students.** ❞
>
> ~Page Keeley
> Former President of NSTA

Available Now

Energy for Teachers of Grades 6–8
Facilitator Guide and Teacher Book Bundle*
Retail: $249.95 • Format: Paperbacks with CD-ROM
ISBN: 978-0-914409-78-6

Force & Motion for Teachers of Grades 6–8
Facilitator Guide and Teacher Book Bundle*
Retail: $249.95 • Format: Paperbacks with CD-ROM
ISBN: 978-0-914409-77-9

Matter for Teachers of Grades 6–8
Facilitator Guide and Teacher Book Bundle*
Retail: $249.95 • Format: Paperbacks with CD-ROM
ISBN: 978-1-938287-02-2

*Teacher Books also sold separately.

Materials in Development
For Teachers of Grades K–8

Organisms
Earth Systems
Plate Tectonics
Weather & Climate

Genes & Traits
Electric Circuits
Sound & Waves

For more information and to order » WestEd.org/mss

or call the WestEd Publications Center » 888.293.7833